JUSTICE IS CONFLICT

JUSTICE IS CONFLICT

Stuart Hampshire

Duckworth

First published in 1999 by
Gerald Duckworth & Co. Ltd.
61 Frith Street, London W1V 5TA
Tel: 0171 434 4242
Fax: 0171 434 4420
Email: duckworth-publishers.co.uk

A catalogue record for this book is available
from the British Library

ISBN 0 7156 2950 6

Typeset by Ray Davies
Printed in Great Britain by
Redwood Books Ltd, Trowbridge

Contents

Preface

At least since 1970 I had been convinced that it was a mistake to look for a moral theory, or a set of propositions, that could serve as a justification, or foundation, of my political loyalties and opinions, which were, and which remain, the opinions of a democratic Socialist. For me, as for many others, the political events of half a century had undermined belief in any discernible direction of historical change, or any known path of human improvement, and it seemed evident to me that my moral notions, and the political attitudes dependent on them, needed to be turned around, and turned toward a thorough-going scepticism and negativity. I came to recognise that my socialist sympathies, and loyalty to the political Left, were far from unreasonable, and not at all difficult to defend, in proportion as they were traceable to emotions engendered by the persisting evils of human life: and poverty in all its modern forms is certainly one of these. My political opinions and loyalties, when challenged, did not any longer include or entail any generalisable account of a future ideal society or of essential human virtues. Rather, they pointed to the possible elimination of particular evils found in particular societies at particular times, and not to universalisable principles of social justice. It is necessary to turn toward the particular case and also toward the negative case, and only then one has sufficient grounds for political action. Arguing for general principles of social justice against traditionalists and conservatives, liberals and reformers had always seemed trapped in circularity, because the conclusions derived from their own arguments supplied the only criterion of rationality and acceptability that they were prepared to accept.

The second motive in revising the account that I give to myself, and to others, of my political sentiments is found in the concept of imagination. By slow steps, and partly from Vico's *Scienza nuova*, and partly from Kant's *Critique of Judgement*, and from my own experience, I came to recognise that the two distinct and complementary functions and forms of thought, imagination and intellect, should always be considered as equals in the context of ethics and politics. This may seem mere common sense in ordinary opinion, but it is not in accordance with the main traditions in political philosophy. The two functions of thought, with their appropriate forms, can be seen as the creative and unmethodical imagination contrasted with the critical and methodical intellect. Conceptions of the good, ideals of social life, visions of individual virtue and excellence, are infinitely various and divisive, rooted in the imagination and in the memories of individuals and in the preserved histories of cities and of states. But the proper business of politics, as Hobbes perceived, is protection against the perennial evils of human life – physical suffering, the destructions and mutilations of war, poverty and starvation, enslavement and humiliation. The protection must be found in universally acceptable rational procedures of negotiation and in the intellectual procedures of adversary reasoning and compromise.

The great evils are truly perennial, and we can read about the mutilations of war, tyrannies, massacres, and starvation described by ancient writers, as if one is reading a twentieth-century newspaper. Such evils, unlike visions of a better social order, are not culture-dependent. They are felt as evils directly and without recourse to the norms of any particular way of life or to any set of moral ideas. The word 'feeling', and the concept of feeling, are indispensable here. There are many evils – for example, the evil of injustice in the distribution of goods – that need to be revealed and certified by argument as evil before they can be felt as evil. On the other hand, the evils of great poverty, and of sickness and physical suffering, and of the misery of bereavement, are immediately felt as evils by any normally responsive person, unless she has perhaps been distracted from natural feeling by some theory that explains them away: for example, as necessary parts of God's design.

Gradually, and in a series of books, I have come to weigh and to appreciate the full force of Hume's dictum – 'Reason both is, and ought to be, the slave of the passions.' Translated into the linguistic idiom of contemporary philosophy, this dictum becomes – 'In moral and political philosophy one is looking for adequate premises from which to infer conclusions already and independently accepted because of one's feelings and sympathies.' It is difficult to acknowledge the bare contingency of personal feeling as the final stopping-point when one is arguing with oneself, or with others, about the ultimate requirements of social justice. But I am now fairly sure that this is the true stopping-point. This book is the outcome, and the prolongation, of these reflections.

I am very grateful to the Trustees of the Tanner Foundation, who established the Tanner Lectures on Human Values, and to Harvard University, which invited me to give the two lectures in this series for the year 1996-97. This book is a greatly expanded version of those lectures.

εἰδέναι χρὴ … δίκην ἔριν

Heracleitus Fragment 80

Acknowledgements

I am grateful for help and encouragement from T.M. Scanlon, Nancy Cartwright, Joshua Cohen, Dennis Thompson, Stephen de Witze, Bernard Williams, Debra Satz, Avishai Margalit, Giorgio Giorgini, and the Western Division of the American Philosophical Association and the Trustees of the Tanner Foundation.

I

The Soul and the City

*

This book's title comes from Heracleitus; but in Book IV of the Republic (439e) Plato makes Socrates tell this story:

> Leontius, the son of Aglaion, as he came up from the Piraeus on the outside of the northern wall, saw the executioner with some corpses lying near him. Leontius felt a strong desire to look at them, but at the same time he was disgusted and turned away. For a time he struggled with himself and covered his face, but then, overcome by his desire, forcing his eyes wide open and rushing towards the corpses
>   – 'Look for yourselves,' he said, 'you evil things: get your fill of the beautiful sight.'

This is a familiar story of conflict and of ambivalence in the mind of an individual. Conflict, and the regulation of it, is the principal subject of this book. In the *Republic*, Plato argued that there is a clear analogy between conflict and justice in the divided minds of individuals and conflict and justice in the class-divided city. In both cases, justice consists in a harmony of the parts or elements, a harmony imposed by reason. I shall argue that Plato is right about the existence of the analogy between the soul and the city and also right that the concept of justice is best explained by this analogy; but I shall argue that justice cannot consist of any kind of harmony or consensus either in the soul or in the city, because there never will be such a harmony, either in the soul or in the city. In order to persuade you of this, I shall have, first, to persuade you to think of reason and of rationality rather differently from Plato, and second, to persuade you to distinguish between justice and fairness in matters of substance and justice and fairness in matters of procedure: my positive conclusion.

I shall try to persuade you that fairness in procedures for resolving conflicts is the fundamental kind of fairness, and that it is acknowledged as a value in most cultures, places, and times: fairness in procedure is an invariable value, a constant in human nature. Justice and fairness in substantial matters, as in the distribution of goods or in the payment of penalties for a crime, will always vary with varying moral outlooks and with varying conceptions of the good. Because there will always be conflicts between conceptions of the good, moral conflict, both in the soul and in the city, there is everywhere a well-recognised need for procedures of conflict resolution, which can replace brute force and domination and tyranny. This is the place of a common rationality of method that holds together both the divided and disruptive self and the

divided and disruptive state. Rationality and substantial justice do not consist in a consensus and a harmony of belief in
the soul and state from which all conflict has been eliminated,
which is Plato's picture of the soul and state. On the opposing and Heraclitean picture, every soul is always the scene of
conflicting tendencies and of divided aims and ambivalences,
and correspondingly, our political enmities in the city or state
will never come to an end while we have diverse life stories
and diverse imaginations.

Plato and Aristotle had their own motives, political as well
as philosophical, for distinguishing different parts of the soul
as on different levels, a hierarchy of higher and lower. They
had their own motives for singling out the reasoning faculty
as constituting (Aristotle, *Nicomachean Ethics* 1169a 2) the
most authoritative and governing element in the soul. Aristotle explicitly makes the political connection here: 'Just as a
city, or any other systematic whole, is most properly identified with the most authoritative or governing element in it,
so it is in a man.' For personal fulfilment and mental stability
we have to ensure that the naturally governing element in the
soul does in fact govern. If we go against nature in this matter
of internal governance, we shall suffer for it. There is no
choice if we are to live successful lives. There is a choice in
the public, external matter – political choice – and the choice
is to be guided by the analogy with natural subordinations
recognised in the soul. It is by analogy that the city can be
said to be a happy or unhappy city in accordance with the

right or wrong political choices being made, with the effect that either a harmonious or a discordant social structure comes into existence.

I suggest that, in reversing this tradition, we start at the other end of the analogy and proceed in the opposite direction: that we start with natural and universal public procedures and institutions which are to be found in all, or in almost all, cities or states. We then explain the processes attributed to the divided soul of a person as based on an analogy with the natural procedures in the city or state. The procedures necessary to any workable social order are to be seen as primary. Mental processes in the minds of individuals are to be seen as the shadows of publicly identifiable procedures that are pervasive across different cultures. Everyday speech helps here. The words that we ordinarily use to distinguish mental processes – 'deliberating', 'judging', 'adjudicating', 'reviewing', 'examining', and many others – have both a public and an inner mental use. The inner mental uses are best explained through reference to the observable public activities. The relations between the public activities of deliberating and adjudicating are open to everyone's observation, and their shadows, the corresponding private mental activities, are assumed to duplicate these relations.

Almost any organised society requires an institution and also a procedure for adjudicating between conflicting moral claims advanced by individuals and by groups within a society. Typically these include claims about property and status, but also conflicts of moral ideals and beliefs, strongly held, that need to be heard and judged, particularly in societies which are not homogeneous in religion, race, custom, and culture.

Second, in any society or state, there needs to be a council or cabinet, even if it is only a council of advisers to the monarch who discuss the various policy options among which a choice has to be made. The typical political case is a choice between war and peace, after discussion, as in Homer's Iliad.

Third, societies and states are liable to suffer disasters and yet to survive: for example, a defeat in a war, or a failure of crops, or an epidemic, or riots and civil disorder. There will need to be some court of inquiry or commission to review rival causal explanations and to assign responsibility as reasonably as possible.

This is a short list of indispensable procedures and institutions that all involve the fair weighting and balancing of contrary arguments bearing on an unavoidable and disputable issue. They are all subject to the single prescription *audi alteram partem* ('hear the other side'). Herbert Hart drew my attention to the centrality of this phrase, defining the principle of adversary argument, when justice is to be done and seen to be done. In each case, the fairness of the public procedure depends as its necessary condition upon this very general prescription being followed.

Discussions in the inner forum of an individual mind

naturally duplicate in form and structure the public adversarial discussions. 'Naturally', because advocates, judges, and diplomats rehearse what they are to say before they step onto the public stage. Anyone who participates in a cabinet discussion, in a law court, in a diplomatic negotiation, acquires the habit of preparing for rebuttals by opponents. He acquires the habit of balanced adversary thinking. The public situations that I have mentioned give rise to corresponding mental processes which are modelled on the public procedures, as a shadowy movement on a ceiling is modelled on an original physical movement on the floor. Moral conflicts are part of every person's experience. In the ever-recurring cases of conflict of principles, adversary argument and then a kind of inner judicial discretion and adjudication are called for.

In private deliberation, the adversary principle of hearing both sides is imposed by the individual on himself as the principle of rationality. 'Hearing' here becomes a metaphor. Most of the verbs that represent thinking are tainted with these metaphors: seeing, weighing, reviewing evidence, and many more. The very notion of a procedure, which I follow in my own mind, is in a sense a metaphorical one. 'Was the proper procedure followed before the decision was made?' is a literal question, admitting a straightforward empirical answer, when it refers to the committee meeting. 'In your own thinking about this, did you follow a proper procedure, reviewing the reasons on both sides, before you made your decision?' addressed to a person, is a less straightforward and a less determinate question. When it is answered, no logbook of the order of mental events is to be expected, and there is no confirmable observation of the procedure that was followed. But the idea of an individual being unbiased, open-minded, and rational in his thinking has sense for us because we know what it is like for a public procedure of discussion to be unbiased, open-minded, and rational. I imagine myself hearing two or more contrary cases presented to me, and I preside over them, allowing the evidence on both sides to be heard; then, and only then, I am to reach a conclusion. This is the process of reflection. One may claim that, whatever the subject matter, this 'hearing the other side'/ *audi alteram partem* is precisely what constitutes thinking in the narrow Cartesian, the methodical, sense of thinking, which identifies thinking with the exercise of the intellect, in contrast to the exercise of imagination. With literary artistry and a sense of drama, Descartes presented the paradigm of thought as a process in the inner consciousness of the solitary thinker, sitting beside his stove, hoping to reconstitute the whole world for himself, as the artificer of his own reality.

I suggest that the Cartesian paradigm should be reversed, and that the paradigmatic setting and circumstance of intellectual thought is not the solitary meditation by the stove but the public arguments for and against some claim publicly made: the supposition is that we learn to transfer, by a kind of mimicry, the adversarial pattern of public and interpersonal life onto a silent stage called the mind. The dialogues are internalised, but they still do not lose the marks of their origin in interpersonal adversarial argument. Viewed in this way, the mind is the unseen and imagined forum into which we learn to project the visible and audible social processes that we first encounter in childhood: practices of asserting, contradicting, deciding, predicting, recalling, approving and disapproving, admiring, blaming, rejecting and accepting, and many more. A child observes the family scenes, the conflicts in which the adults around him discuss and decide, assert and contradict each other, and he soon finds no difficulty in a solitary imitation of these exchanges. Any person hears the different kinds of dialogue as regular forms of behaviour and quickly recognises both the subtle and the gross differences among the types of public dialogue occurring in typical social situations.

Rationality, adversarial thinking, public and private, is properly contrasted with imaginative thinking. Evidently there are many situations requiring careful thought in which adversary arguments are not essential. A painter or musician or poet may not weigh adversary arguments in deciding how a particular work should proceed. If one finds oneself strongly moved and excited by some stretch of the countryside, and finds it beautiful, one is not normally prepared to enter into some adversary argument about its beauty. There seems to be nothing to be gained by one's being just and fair-minded and rational in supporting such a claim, or in insisting on a justification, if someone disagrees and finds the landscape dull. The acceptability of an aesthetic claim is independent of any argumentative procedure associated with the claim, and does not normally require negotiation or arbitration.

Compare the institutions that have given sense to the traditional concept of reason and of intellect as opposed to imagination: they are, first of all, theoretical studies, the study of mathematics, and of logic; and the natural sciences; last, practical studies, the law, and the development of legal systems. The Platonic ordering of disciplines makes mathematical proof the paradigm of reasoning and of rationality. This Platonic concept of reason is not the only possible one, and for some purposes, such as understanding the nature of justice and of morality, it has been greatly misleading.

Turn it upside down. What is gained by representing the concept of rationality as having its origins in the adversary reasoning typical of legal and moral disputes and disputes about evidence, rather than in the formal deductions and proofs that are characteristic of logic and mathematics? The first advantage is that an account can be given of how a common norm of rationality develops naturally from necessities of social life; that is, from the inevitably recurrent conflicts which must be resolved if communities are to survive. On the other hand, the notion of pure reason, the eternal and governing part of the soul, is a theory without explanatory value. Second, if the paradigm of rationality is taken to be deductive inference, the norm of rationality as applied to prudential and historical reasoning, and to legal and moral reasoning, will then seem to be utterly disconnected, as indeed sceptics have always argued that they are. There then seems to be no link between the form of reasoning that issues in the necessary truths of mathematics and forms of reasoning that issue in moral judgements, legal judgements, or judgements of private or public prudence. The link is the familiar notions of rationality and of argument.

Throughout history, the concept of justice has always been linked with the concepts of rationality and of reasonableness. Many philosophers and theologians within the natural law tradition have attributed to the supposed faculty of pure reason the capacity to discriminate relationships that are substantially just and reasonable, and in accordance with principles of equity, from those that are not. According to this natural law tradition, reason by itself discerns that the connection between justice and the protection of property is a necessary connection, like the connection between being a three-sided plane figure and being a three-angled plane figure. Yet the theorists of natural law have never ceased to hear in the background the subversive whispers of the sceptics, suggesting that there certainly have been, and probably will continue to be, social orders in which these supposed universal connections have no hold on intelligent persons' minds, and in which property rights are thought of, not as necessary and universal, but as contingent and as dependent upon specific social conditions and local circumstances.

From this ancient and still continuing philosophical conflict, one conclusion can safely be drawn: that it is useless and self-defeating to conduct the discussion in psychological terms; that is, in terms of the parts of the soul, or of powers of mind – useless, because it is always inconclusive. Each side in the argument invents a philosophy of mind, a division of the parts of the soul, that is designed to support its thesis about justice, and consequently the argument goes round and round in a circle. If the argument is removed from the shadowy mental realm into the open world of institutions and practices, as these are studied by historians and by anthropologists, a determinate answer, or at least a clarification of the dispute, becomes possible. We can begin to see both why the absolute conception of justice has often seemed indispensable and why the relativist conception of justice has often seemed unavoidable. Particular institutions, each with its specific procedures for deciding between rival conceptions of what is substantially just and fair, come and go in history. The one most general feature of the processes of decision is preserved as the necessary condition that qualifies a process, whatever it happens to be, to be accounted as an essentially just and fair one: that contrary claims are heard. An unjust procedure, violating this necessary condition of procedural fairness, is unjust, always and everywhere and without reference to any distinct conception of the good.

In any adversary procedure, the normal case is the man who from the beginning of his adult life finds himself attached to an ethnic group, a social group, a locality, perhaps a religious or moral group, and where each group is in competition with other groups for some degree of dominance in a single society. In such conditions of competition there are two routes by which a person or group may seek to gain its ends: by outright domination, involving force and the threat of force, or, alternatively, by an argumentative procedure within some institution (parliament, law court, assembly) that happens to have come into existence with its own recognised rules of procedure. The existence of such an institution for adversary argument is the second necessary condition of a just procedure.

The existence of such an institution, and the particular form of its rules and conventions of procedure, are matters of historical contingency. There is no rational necessity about the more specific rules and conventions determining the criteria for success in argument in any particular institution, except the overriding necessity that each side in the conflict should be heard putting its case.

At a less thoughtful level, and without the civility of argument, a duel fought to resolve a quarrel can be fair, in virtue of its procedures, while an ambush or mere affray makes no pretence of fairness. There is no prescribed procedure. The idea of equal opportunity for both sides, that is, the idea of procedural justice, governs the rituals of the traditional duel with swords or pistols, and of many other kinds of traditional contest and ordeals. Neither side must be allowed within the duel an unfair advantage, and the only inequality must come from the temperament and the skill of the individuals involved. A duel obviously presents only a partial analogy to adversary reasoning in a law court or parliament, but it is a very clear example of an institution for conflict resolution governed by traditional rules and rituals, and also by an ideal of fairness in procedure. To be killed in a duel, as were Pushkin and Lassalle, is different, and it has always been felt to be different, from just being killed in a pub brawl, as was Christopher Marlowe.

In the silent thought of any individual, rationality is best characterised as two-sided reflection. When the evidences to be surveyed and evaluated, the objects of reflection, are the subject's own conflicting desires and feelings, she would not expect to be reliably controlled in her final judgement by some clear and well-established procedure. Our desires, sentiments, attitudes, and intentions normally compose an unstable and confused scene in our minds, with all the ambivalences and contradictions that the story of Leontius illustrates.

We do not know anything about reason as a faculty, apart from what philosophers and theologians and others have chosen to put into the concept. Parts of the soul, unlike arms and legs, are a philosophical invention. Here are some of the typical activities that can be grouped together as activities of adversary reasoning, and of the intellect as contrasted with imagination: the weighing of evidence for and against a hypothesis in a social science; the weighing of evidence in a historical or criminal investigation or in civil litigation; and the whole sphere of public prudence and policy-formation. Different skills are required in each of these activities, but they can be grouped together as reasoning in conditions of uncertainty. Consider a strongly contrasting list of natural and thoughtful human activities that we expect to find in all societies in some form or other: and they are the activities of the imagination – storytelling, poetry, music, drama, visual art, public celebrations, the description of ideal societies and ideal persons and ideal ways of life, and moral imagination. These are activities that we expect to vary vastly in form and content in different places, in different social groups, at different times in history, and in distinguishable cultures. We not only expect the diversity; we positively demand it. Their diversity, like that of the natural languages, helps to establish the identity of distinct populations and of cultures.

The first set of activities have been wrongly accorded a superior station on the ground that they distinguish humanity from the beasts in the multilevelled soul. Both lists of activities distinguish humanity from the beasts. The difference is elsewhere. Activities of reason in the first list unite humanity in shared and identical pursuits and procedures. The thought required is convergent. The second list consists of activities that tend to divide humanity into distinct groups, each with their own languages, customs, rituals, arts, and moral ideas. The thought is divergent and particularised. The activities in the first list do not change their form as they are spread across frontiers. Even more strictly convergent is the reasoning in logic and mathematics, crossing all frontiers. But for social customs, moral ideals, rituals, liturgies, celebrations, music, poetry, and visual art, we do not expect universal criteria of evaluation; rather, they help to distinguish different ways of life. They also divide persons in accordance with temperament and taste: Javanese music can be enjoyed in Germany, but Javanese music is not expected to have the qualities of German music. Beethoven is enjoyed in China, but his procedures of composition, his style, are not those of Chinese music; no convergence is here to be expected or desired. Within the same population, we all have sharply different allergies and repugnances.

Conflict, social and psychological, was the great evil for Plato and Aristotle. From the stratification of classes in the city, each playing its own role, a satisfying harmony is to arise, and that harmony defines social justice. Similarly with the governance of an individual soul. Individuals cannot fall into painful inner conflict if in each of them personal ideas, desires, emotions, and habits of feeling are governed by certain knowledge of fixed norms and principles. This picture of a possible harmony under the governance of reason is carried through the Christian centuries and persists in the philosophy of the Enlightenment, and it persists in contemporary liberalism also. Whatever the contingent differences between us arising from our personal history – from our memories and imagination – the king in his castle and the peasant in his hovel are one, in their common humanity, in virtue of the overriding superiority of rational moral principles that king and peasant both implicitly recognise.

Professor John Rawls revived the study of political philosophy by taking one necessary step away from this traditional search for harmony. In *A Theory of Justice*, he declared that his rationally chosen principles of justice must be independent of conceptions of the good. But he has also acknowledged that his principles are to be rationally chosen specifically by those who live in a liberal and democratic society, where they may represent an overlapping political consensus about the principles of substantial justice. Once again, there is harmony, but harmony within the liberal stockade. Someone whose conception of good and evil is founded on a supernatural authority, which represents any tolerance of a contrary moral view as evil, will not, for example, accept the primacy of liberty. In any truly liberal society such illiberal persons are to be expected. This confinement of reasonably acceptable principles of justice to liberal and democratic societies bypasses the outstanding political problem of our time, which is the relation between two kinds of society: on the one hand, self-consciously traditional societies and governments, where priests of the church or rabbis or imams or mullahs, and other experts in the will of God, maintain a single conception of the good that determines the way of life of the society as a whole; and on the other hand, the liberal democratic societies and governments that permit, or encourage, a plurality of conceptions of the good. The severity of this confrontation was for a long time concealed by the belief in a positivist theory of modernisation. The positivists believed that all societies across the globe would gradually discard their traditional attachments to supernatural forces because of the need for rational, scientific, and experimental methods of thought which a modern industrial economy involves. This is the old faith, widespread in the nineteenth century, that there must be a step-by-step convergence on liberal values, on 'our values'.

We now know that there is no 'must' about it, and that all such general theories of human history have a predictive value near to zero. They are just diachronic versions of the Platonic and Marxist belief in a final rational harmony. It is not only possible but, on present evidence, probable that most conceptions of the good and most ways of life which are typical of commercial, liberal, industrialised societies, will often seem altogether hateful to substantial minorities within these societies, and even more hateful to most of the populations within traditional societies elsewhere. As a liberal, I think I ought to expect to be found superficial by a large part of mankind, both at home and abroad. One needs to see that one's own way of life, and habits of speech and of thought, not only seem wrong to large populations, but can be repugnant in very much the same way in which alien habits of eating, or alien sexual customs, can be repugnant.

Liberals such as Professor Rawls and I believe that there is no great moral significance to be attached to the accident of our place of birth and of our inheritance. Our moral opponents, whom liberals sometimes call fanatics, see destiny, intention, or design in their inheritance, and from their ancestry they infer a very specific mission, a specific set of duties, and a clear plan for their lives. Perhaps this most fundamental of all oppositions in politics comes from contrasting attitudes to time, historical time. When, famously, 'Remember 1689' is chalked on a wall in Belfast by a Roman Catholic calling to mind William III's Protestant Settlements, it would most certainly be useless to respond 'Be fair and reasonable: forget the injustices of the past, as you see them, because the past cannot now be repaired; it is more fair and reasonable to start from now and to try to build a peaceful society for the future.' The response comes back: 'You are asking us to forget who we are. Like everyone else, we define ourselves by what we reject. We should cease to exist as a community if we thought only of the future and of what you call reasonableness. That would be disintegration, the loss of integrity, both as individuals and as a community.' Self-definition by opposition is the moral equivalent of the old logical principle *Omnis determinatio est negatio*.

I. *The Soul and the City*

Procedures of conflict resolution within any state are always being criticised and are always changing and are never as fair and as unbiased as they ideally might be. But if they are well known and are a part of a continuous history, they are acceptable for reasons that Hume explained in his essay 'The Ideal Commonwealth'. The institutions and their rituals hold society together, insofar as they are successful and well established in the resolution of moral and political conflicts according to particular local and national conventions: 'this is our peculiar form of governance and we cling to it.'

This is justice and fairness in procedures - whether in duels, sports, games, law courts, parliaments, in all kinds of arguments and in adversary processes in which one side wins and another side loses, either fairly or unfairly. That is how politics and social life for the most part go forward, at best in controlled and recognised conflicts, sometimes enjoyably, sometimes painfully.

Looking back, we can criticise, from a moral point of view, historical institutions such as slavery in the American south, the subordination of women in Victorian England, and the caste system in India, as substantially unjust, while explaining and defending the liberal conception of substantial justice, which has emerged gradually in Europe and America as the outcome of past conflicts. We may also criticise the distribution of wealth and of income in America or Britain today as grossly and substantially unjust, also in the light of a particular conception of distributive justice, which is part of a whole moral outlook and of a particular conception of the good. In this case, we will expect opposition from conservatives, who have another conception of justice that they can defend and that is part of their conception of good, stressing property rights and the autonomy of individuals.

The issue of distributive justice so far remains abstract, theoretical, and indeterminate. When there is an actual political confrontation with economic conservatives on one side and economic reformers on the liberal side, the ensuing argument assumes the existence of some of the institutions and customs prevailing at that time and place. The participants in the conflict are no longer considering the abstract question of whether the present actual distribution of wealth can be considered just or unjust, taken in isolation from the other institutions of the time and place, and in an ideal and imaginary social world, started from scratch: the Shelleyan stance. I am assuming that each is making his own case in the real world of necessary politics, following the customary and rule-governed procedures of public argument and decision-making appropriate to such cases in this particular society. The specific forms of argument and negotiation, and the arenas in which the conflicts are to be fought out, are often themselves subjects of dispute as much as the substantial conceptions of justice involved. Like substantial conceptions of justice, the vehicles of dispute are expected to change as the untidy upshot of regular political conflicts. The second-order and procedural questions have to be made the subject of political conflict and negotiation. The framework of such a political dispute, if it is handled with justice and fairness, is still the universal principle of adversary argument.

Whatever a person's moral outlook and conception of the good, and whatever his beliefs about issues of substantial justice, he knows that he will sometimes collide with others who make contrary judgements. Unless he is a hermit, he will find himself to some extent constrained by certain nearly universal habits of argumentative behaviour that can be collectively called the habit of playing the game of argument according to the locally appropriate rules. In childhood, he learned to involve himself in the institutionalised games and contests that his coevals played, accepting in the process the historically contingent rules which defined these games. When he grew older, he naturally realised that, if he had been born elsewhere and in another century, he would have been involved in different institutions, different contests. But the nature of the involvement, and of the innate disposition to join in, would have been the same.

Because of this alternation between necessity and contingency, philosophical theory has always traced an uncertain and wavering path between ethical relativism on the one hand and ethical absolutism on the other. In times and places where there was slavery, there were rules and conventions governing the fair and just treatment of slaves. In some of these places and at some of these times, there were those who thought that these rules and conventions were wholly inadequate from the standpoint of substantial justice in the treatment of human beings, and who came finally to denounce the whole institution of slavery as always in substance unjust. Similarly, I can remember from my childhood in the 1920s that domestic servants in England were at that time helpless if, after a quarrel, their employers refused to give them a reference. They were doomed to unemployment. Most people now would probably consider this dependence and helplessness to be grossly unjust, but ordinary opinion at the time did not recognise the injustice.

In my time class-conflict, stirred up by a self-conscious labour movement, has led to new ideas of substantial justice. The imaginative and radical critics of established conceptions of substantial justice repeatedly widen the debate and open up cases of injustice that had hitherto been beyond the range of discussion. So in the past with criticism of unregulated factory labour, of inequality between the sexes, of limited voting rights, of unequal access to health care, of unequal access to education, unequal access to legal aid. Moral imagination engenders new conflicts with new conceptions of the good, when it coincides with some social unrest, which is malleable and can be directed.

All modern societies are, to a greater or lesser degree, morally mixed, with rival conceptions of justice, conservative and radical, flaring into open conflict and needing arbitration. In the extreme case obviously the conflicts break through all procedural restraints into violence. No state will realise a perfect fairness in the representation of the conflicting moral outlooks within it. A continuing approximation to contemporary ideals of fairness in resolving conflicts, and new institutions that tend to redress the more blatant inequalities, are the best that can be expected. Procedural justice tends of its nature to be imperfect and not ideal, being the untidy outcome of past political compromises. What emerges from a fair political contest will often be described by those who are intent on a specific form of substantial justice as 'a shabby compromise'.

For the individual also, as for society, compromise, shabby or smart, is certainly the normal, and often the most desirable, condition of the soul for a creature whose desires and emotions are usually ambivalent and always in conflict with each other. A smart compromise is one where the tension between contrary forces and impulses, pulling against each other, is perceptible and vivid, and both forces and impulses have been kept at full strength: with the tension of the Heraclitean bow. An example would be a singer's effort to hold together in her singing complete technical control with complete spontaneity of expression. This unresolved tension of opposites is felt in excellent musical performances and in great works of art and literature. We do not normally live like this, with sustained and undiminished tension, whether as individuals or as communities. We are not masterpieces in our lives, and the lives of communities are not master classes. We look for some relaxation of tension, but, until death, we do not expect the neat disappearance of conflict and of tension, whether in the soul or in society. As individuals, our lives will turn out in retrospect to be a rough and running compromise between contrary ambitions, and the institutions that survive in the state have usually been cobbled together in the settlement of some long past conflicts, probably now forgotten.

Neither in a social order, nor in the experience of an individual, is a state of conflict the sign of a vice, or a defect, or a malfunctioning. It is not a deviation from the normal state of a city or of a nation, and it is not a deviation from the normal course of a person's experience. To follow through the ethical implications of these propositions about the normality of conflict, these Heraclitean truths, a kind of moral conversion is needed, a new way of looking at all the virtues, including the virtue of justice. We need to turn around the mirror of theory, so that we see ourselves both as we are and as we have been.

Several contemporary moral philosophers have argued that there will always be a plurality of different and incompatible conceptions of the good, and that there cannot be a single comprehensive and consistent theory of human virtue: for instance, Isaiah Berlin made this point in an essay on Machiavelli, who had insisted on the incompatibility of Christian innocence with political success and security. But my slogan here, 'all determination is negation', is intended to present a stronger thesis: the superior power of the negative. Most influential conceptions of the good have defined themselves as rejections of their rivals: for instance, some of the ideals of monasticism were a rejection of the splendours and hierarchies of the Church, and this rejection was part of the original sense and purpose of the monastic ideal. Some forms of fundamentalism, both Christian and others, define themselves as a principled rejection of secular, liberal, and permissive moralities. Fundamentalism is the negation of any deviance in moral opinion, and of the very notion of opinion in ethics.

The essence of a liberal morality is the rejection of any final and exclusive authority, natural or supernatural, and of the accompanying compulsion and censorship. In this context, freedom itself is felt, and is cherished, as a negative notion: no walls of dogma, no unquestionable rules from priests and politicians; the future is to be an open field for discovery. Openness is a negative concept, appropriately therefore an indeterminate concept. The liberal's adversary is disgusted, or made nervous, by this negativity, by the openness and the emptiness, by the looseness of undirected living. The ensuring conflict is stark and often bitter. Only in communities that flourished before modern communications existed could citizens possibly have been ignorant of systems of reflective moral belief that were odious in their eyes. Now they might reasonably, recognising the confrontation, come together in ranking political activities, the skilful management of conflicts, as among the highest of human skills. On the other hand, it does not follow from the fact that procedural justice is defined by a universal principle, a principle of rationality, that it must override all other moral considerations in everybody's mind. Men and women generally recognise that there may be some exceptional circumstances in which they will hold that considerations of procedural justice and of rationality ought to be overridden in order that some other essential value which is dominant in their morality may be protected, such as the avoidance of widespread misery or the preservation of life.

There normally is in any modern society a chaos of opinions and of moral attitudes. A reasonable person knows that there is this chaos, and those with strong opinions, or with fanatical hearts, deplore the chaos and hope for a consensus: usually for a consensus in which their own opinions and attitudes are dominant. A socialist by conviction, I consider poverty alongside great wealth a great and unnecessary evil and a substantial injustice, and I expect a continuing political fight with those whose conception of the good and whose idea of fairness is an incompatible one. This is the proper domain of politics. There will be, on one side, the well-trained rhetoric of conservative thinking, and on the other the rhetoric of radical reform and redistribution.

In many essential respects the metaethical theory I have been assuming is close to Hume's: that opinions about substantial justice and the other virtues arise from, and are explained by, natural and widespread human sentiments greatly modified by very variable customs and social histories. But in the classical tradition Hume still believed that humanity has a tendency toward a consensus in its moral sentiments. After he has dismissed the claims of reason to guarantee general agreement in morality, he reintroduced the goal of harmony and consensus through the idea of a constant human nature governing our sentiments and sympathies. I have been arguing that the diversity and divisiveness of languages and of cultures and of local loyalties is not a superficial but an essential and deep feature of human nature – both unavoidable and desirable – rooted in our divergent imaginations and memories. More fundamentally, our stronger sentiments are exclusive and immediately lead to competition and conflict, because our memories, and with them our imagination, are focused upon particular persons, particular inherited languages, particular places, particular social groups, particular rituals and religions, and particular tones of voice; and hence our stronger loyalties are similarly focused. We want to serve and to reinforce the particular institutions that protect us, and to extend their power and influence at the expense of their rivals.

This philosophy of conflict can be pressed further in a metaphysical vein. The individuality of any active thing depends upon its power to resist the invasion and dominance of the active things around it. This is the metaphysical principle that Spinoza thought must apply to all things within the natural order and therefore to all persons and identifiable groups in the civil order also. Men and women are naturally driven to resist any external force that tends to repress their typical activities or to limit their freedom. This is true of individuals, families, social classes, religious groups, ethnic groups, nations. This is the common order of nature. They are all, these different units, struggling, wittingly or unwittingly, to preserve their individual character and their distinctive qualities against the encroachment and absorption of other self-assertive things in their environment. Given this picture of the natural order, diversity, rather than conformity, is not a moral prescription, as Mill thought, one option among others. It is a natural necessity for each distinct entity to try to preserve its distinctiveness for as long as it can, and for this reason conflicts are at all times to be expected in the history of individuals, of social groups, and of nations, as their paths intersect. There is no end to conflict within and around the civil order.

This is a metaphysical vision, a speculation. Spinoza's picture is of unavoidable conflicts of interest in the pursuit of survival. But it can apply also to conflicts between conceptions of the good with which people are passionately identified. The evidence of personal experience and of political history is strong in support of this picture. Every person recognises the exclusiveness of many of his emotions, which make him turn his back on other emotions and interests that he knows also have a claim on him. The normal state of a person with normally strong feelings is like Leontius's state of mind, with which I began.

In the context of international affairs, it is now evident that the human race is unlikely to survive for very long unless reasonably fair procedures develop and become accepted for negotiations and arbitrations in the settling of international conflicts threatening war. My argument is relevant, first, in its suggestion that bringing into existence institutions and recognised procedures should have priority over declarations of universal principles; second, in its suggestion that institutions earn respect mainly from their customary use and from their gradually acquired familiarity. There is a chance that a kind of case law will step-by-step develop within disarmament negotiations and through them a rough sense of fairness in the adjudication of conflicts, always given equality of access: not perfect fairness, but the kind of imperfect fairness that may emerge from procedures which are themselves compromises, from the relicts of history. Nothing more is reasonably to be expected.

Rationality, prudential and moral, as a common human possession or potentiality, is most plausibly identified, as argument and counterargument, with the just and fair weighing of conflicts of evidence, and of conflicts of desires. Every individual person has used procedures for resolving contrary pulls and contrary impulses: political conflicts and their resolution are strictly analogous.

In the political arena I will defend those institutions which contribute to the realisation of my conception of the good, and which protect my conception of substantial justice from its enemies. My requirement from my moral enemies is the requirement that I impose upon myself: that contrary views of what is just and fair are allowed equal hearing, equal access, in the city or state, and that no one conception of substantial justice in society is imposed by domination and by the threat of force. What do I do when a rival conception of the good leaves no place for procedural justice, and when it will not recognise fairness in the settlement of disputes as a virtue? This is the bind in which liberal and nonauthoritarian morality is apt to find itself: if a particular conception of the good does not already include the virtue of respect for fairness in procedure, and for rationality in this procedural sense, where does this independent and indispensable virtue find its authority and justification?

The authority and the justification are to be found in the structure of practical reason itself. This is my thesis: it is a kind of transcendental argument. Everyone uses the balancing of pros and cons in his own mind in the pursuit of his own conception of the good, as well as in common prudence, in pursuit of his own interests.

Our various conceptions of the good are formed, in the last resort and at the end of all tests for consistency, by our perceptions and by our imagination, which in turn determine our feelings. In the Christian era, we have confused ourselves by allowing our imaginations to gallop along two contrary paths. The first is the path of the monotheists, one God, creator, and arbiter. Obviously, if one God, only one morality – His law and the falsity of moral pluralism therefore. The other is the path trodden by Herodotus: the historical consciousness, glorying in the variety of ways of life and in the imagination of them. This glory was associated with the pagan polytheism which could respect many tutelary gods, each in his or her particular place. Sacredness and reverence were diffused, and the contrast between the Athenians and Spartans, in their ideals of humanity, was a glory both of them.

Looking back to Herodotus and to Plato, and to the slave economies of the ancient world, one must not be so carried away by the moral differences between now and then as to forget the greater identities. There remain the unchanged horrors of human life, the savage and obvious evils, which scarcely vary from culture to culture or from age to age: massacre, starvation, imprisonment, torture, death and mutilation in war, tyranny and humiliation – in fact, the evening and the morning news. Whatever the divergences in conceptions of the good, these primary evils stay constant and undeniable as evils to be at all costs averted, or almost all costs. One matching constant on the positive side is common everyday rationality, the power of argument – a weak protection, you may say, and that is why I am a pessimist.

The ground for hope is the thought that the sphere of political action may be gradually extended as more of the great evils, such as starvation and poverty, are moved from the column headed 'natural misfortunes' into the column headed 'political failures'. This has regularly happened in the past, as with chattel slavery and the subordination of women, and it can happen again with poverty and famine. The perpetual conflict between conservative thinking, in all its varieties, and the ambitions of reformers, socialists, and liberals comes, in the last analysis, from this single source: ought we to raise continually our consciousness of political possibilities, or ought we to accept the limits of political agency that, as it happens, our history has so far left in place? In any period the rhetoric of freedom displays pride in human agency, even if it is only the agency of a Renaissance prince: the opposing rhetoric of conservatism displays pride in the steadiness and continuity of social practices and of old forms of life. In any particular conflict of values, this confrontation is liable to be tinged with real hostility and depth of feeling, because incompatible conceptions of the good are at stake. In fact, incompatible conceptions of evil would be a more realistic phrase for moral values, because a moral outlook or theory is usually best defined by its exclusions and prohibitions.

Alongside conflicting moral traditions within a single society there can at the same time be a shared political culture within shared institutions. Those who operate within the various institutions in pursuit of their own particular ends naturally come to share certain professional attitudes and customs, and a common professional morality. The word 'community' is much used in political philosophy. I think the true communities in modern life are to be found in professions and shared pursuits, in the communities of people who work together. Most lawyers, most actors, most soldiers and sailors, most athletes, most doctors, and most diplomats feel a certain solidarity in the face of outsiders, and, in spite of other differences, they share fragments of a common ethic in their working life, and a kind of moral complicity. The same is true of politicians in a democratic, or halfway democratic, state, which will generate a cadre of professional politicians who, through all their hostilities, recognise their similarities of habit. It is entirely normal that these moral cross-currents should be strongly felt: one may dislike a class of persons for their seeming indifference to social justice and to ordinary fairness, as one conceives them, and at the same time share with them a common political culture and a respect for the procedures that will elaborately manage these hostilities. Human beings are not consistent in their emotions, in their alliances and enmities, in accordance with some simple model of consistency. This is the positive side of ambivalences and of ambiguities of feeling.

Engagement in contests of all kinds comes naturally to us and is a large part of the stuff of everyday experience. I anticipate the comment that I am representing procedural justice as only the English notion of fair play, with politics as a form of game. This comment is unfair and unhistorical.

The idea of a fair contest goes far back in time and has multiple roots in pre-Christian ages and more particularly in classical pagan cultures. We have to rid ourselves of a too streamlined model of the human mind and of its inbuilt contrarieties of feeling. Respect for a process can, as a matter of habit, coexist with detestation of the outcome of the process, and this particularly in democracies.

My argument about the two kinds of justice is supposed to be entirely general, with ballot-box democracy one kind of government among others. Democracy has usually been advocated as the form of government that will ensure the most complete and fair representation of all citizens of the state, as far as this is possible. The implication is that the more democratic the state is in this sense the better, because it is a good thing that the most popular policy, the most strongly supported, should prevail. This is a substantial moral claim, perhaps to be further defended by some specific theory of freedom or of natural rights. But I see no reason myself to accept this claim. When a majority, following a natural tendency, advocates wrong policies – perhaps in the punishment of crime, in the treatment of ethnic minorities, in immigration policy, in foreign policy, and elsewhere – the popularity of the policies cannot for me, for my conception of the good, mitigate the errors and the evil. The value of a democratic constitution lies in the defence of minorities, not of majorities. One needs to ensure, for the sake of justice, that the minorities are properly heard and that they play their necessary part in the process. I and my political allies will often be on the losing side. If in a democracy we happen to have the power to frustrate the justly established will of the majority, it would be evidently unfair and unjust of us to do so, unless we are convinced that the policy chosen is so overwhelmingly evil and destructive as to override the claims of procedural justice. Otherwise we will sadly follow the democratic rules, expecting our adversaries to have an equally strong feeling for rationality and just procedures when we happen to win and they happen to lose.

Conflict is perpetual: why then should we be deceived?

II

Against Monotheism

*

There are other reasons for denying the possibility of eliminating fundamental moral conflicts from modern societies, to be added to the reasons that I have suggested in the preceding chapter. An aggressively secular and liberal morality, which stands in the tradition established by John Stuart Mill, first, rejects all supernatural sources of moral authority and of moral knowledge, and, second, denies, more specifically, that there exists a God, the Creator, who has communicated to humanity his plans for humanity and hence has supplied a set of moral prescriptions flowing from these plans. At least in the West there has been no tradition of accepting some supernatural warrant or guarantee of the legitimacy of moral distinctions while denying the existence of one God, whether God as conceived by Christians, Jews, or Muslims.

Those who accept the thesis of monotheism will believe that all mankind is subject to the same moral constraints, and that only one conception of the good is finally acceptable. Even if it does not become a positive duty to proselytise, as Christian missionaries do, and to act politically in support of the one authoritative conception of the good, such believers cannot consistently accept that many different conceptions of the good are, or in principle may be, defensible. I evidently reject monotheism and a supernatural authority in ethics. I am arguing that, if, we are to proselytise at all, it ought to be in the interest of denying the claim to universality of all substantive creeds, and of advocating fairness in handling the conflicts between the creeds. The primary enemy from my standpoint is monotheism, and after that, moral universalism such as the utilitarian philosophy, which, in its classical form, submerged the salient differences of aspiration among individuals and among societies in a single, highly abstract principle of action, and in the pursuit of a single value: pleasure and the avoidance of pain. The opposite of monotheism and of this monomoralism is the recognition of polymorphous ideals and of diverse conceptions of the good, tempered by respect for the local conventions and rules of conflict resolution. It is reasonable to be a universalist in the cause of reasonableness in the regulation of conflicts ('hear the other side'), but not a universalist in the defence of particular outcomes of particular conflicts of moral opinion.

Fairness and justice in procedures are the only virtues that can reasonably be considered as setting norms to be universally respected. The claim to universal respect is founded upon the antecedent claim of rationality to universal respect; and this claim in turn is founded on, and is supported by, a universal feature of human behaviour: the habit of adversary reasoning in conditions of uncertainty, the equal attention to arguments pro and con before a conclusion is accepted. The norm of fairness and justice in the resolution of social conflicts is directly derived from the weighing of evidence, which is required in the gathering of knowledge, whether in historical studies, or in the sciences, or in practical common sense. But this appeal to a universal norm, the norm of rationality in argument, is entirely abstract and general, until another norm, which is also constitutive of the idea of a just procedure of conflict resolution, comes into play: no procedure is considered fair and just, anywhere and at any time, unless the particular procedure employed is chosen to be, or to become, the regular one. This necessary condition of fairness in the resolution of conflicts can claim to be universally recognised because it also is derivable from a universal, or nearly universal, feature of human behaviour. Human beings are habituated to recognise the rules and conventions of the institutions within which they have been brought up, including the conventions of their family life. Institutions are needed as settings for just procedures of conflict resolution, and institutions are formed by recognised customs and habits, which harden into specific rules of procedure within the various institutions – law courts, parliaments, councils, political parties, and others. The members of any society, and the citizens of any state, at any time and anywhere, normally expect that the conflicts in which they are involved should be settled in accordance with the rules recognised within that particular society or that particular state.

Evidently there exist at any time in a society or state many different types of institution adapted to different types of conflict. Fairness in advocacy is different from fairness in adjudication: fairness in parliament and in party politics is different from fairness in a law court and in an arbitration. The local institutions, each with its peculiar history, customs, and conventions, will specify the typical forms of fairness and evenhandedness established in the particular institutions. The plurality of forms of institution extends across the plurality of types of conflict. Therefore the requirements of procedural justice vary immensely in different places and at different times in virtue of local customs and rules. All the diverse customs and conventions are recognised to be subordinate to a common and very general purpose – the just and fair weighing of conflicting policies, proposals, or opinions. In the domain of procedural justice we can uniquely combine the advantages of an element of universality with an element of diversity: the procedures must admit, as a universal requirement, a fair hearing to the two or more sides in a conflict, and at the same time the institutions involved in the resolution of conflicts must have earned, or be earning, respect and recognition from their history in a particular state or society. Therefore procedural justice shares at least one feature with substantive justice: that one needs to refer to the social situation and beliefs and traditions of the particular society at the particular time in order to determine whether the resolution of a particular conflict is, or was, just or fair. Perhaps the procedures employed were not as ideally fair and even-handed as could be imagined, perhaps because they were arrived at as compromises after some contests in the past when the procedural issues were first disputed; but they may well have been fair enough by ordinary standards.

If one starts to evaluate political institutions, social customs and conventions, legal institutions, and common conceptions of fairness, in this historical spirit, with attention to the conflicts from which they have emerged, one will be less inclined to attribute their survival to that abstract and loose entity called 'human nature'. Hume believed that the stability and endurance of an institution or custom, or of a set of moral attitudes, is sufficient evidence that they conform to human nature, and that a priori criticism of them from some ideal moral point of view is usually out of place and futile. He implied a parallel between uniformities prevailing in human nature, the habits of the mind, and the laws of Newtonian physics. By this argument the sheer contingency, even the chanciness, of widespread and well-established moral attitudes, institutions, and customs are overlooked. Anomalous customs often prove permanent. One is left by Hume with the suggestion that there is a kind of necessity attached to our widespread and stable moral attitudes, institutions, and customs, although it is not rational necessity but the necessity of natural law, the laws of human psychology.

But a historian, and Hume wrote history, has a different story to tell when he comes to account for widespread and enduring attitudes in a particular country to social justice, and to laws of poverty, and to the Church, and to religion in general, and to parliament and the monarchy, and to sexual and family customs, and to foreign wars, and to the specific forms of common courtesy. His narrative will trace the path that leads past accidents of battle in wars of religion and wars of ideology, and past the accidents of personality and of individual passion, up to the present relative stability and to the apparent standstill. Having looked back across the contingencies, he will not be inclined to interpret contemporary political and social institutions, in Britain or France or the United States, as 'natural' in any deep and serious sense. The bland surface of inherited institutions, customs, and conventions does not altogether smother traces of the many dispersed contests and conflicts that finally subsided and were at least temporarily resolved. The historically minded person will therefore be ready to expect the now unexpected breakup of the apparently stable surface of institutions because of some unanticipated change in the surrounding circumstances. Many future contingencies will allow the future to be changed by political action before any limits set by 'human nature' are encountered. The subordination of women, in political and social life and in employment, seemed the most natural of customs, responding to the obvious needs of human nature, as it seemed, until other changes in social relations, and perhaps also some imaginative advocacy, undermined the accepted common sense of things at this particular point.

The cardinal error, the trap, is to project the more stable and widespread habits and conventions of a particular time and place into an abstract model and then to call this model 'human nature'. This abstract model of human nature may for a time be roughly adequate for ordinary planning purposes, representing, as it may, the general run of shared moral attitudes up to the present time with all exceptions and minor deviations left out. The error is to take the abstract model as the entire and literal truth, or to suppose that it corresponds to the many diverse actual feelings, attitudes, and conventions in the observed world. Its very tidiness, and the fact that it can be comprehended in a single vision, suggest that there is no such correspondence.

Note a contrast: Newton's laws of motion explained and predicted the interrelations of the observed heavenly bodies with an accuracy and completeness that astonished the learned world. It was as if nature had presented itself to our observation in the guise of an abstract model. There was a satisfying fit between the clear conceptual scheme, with the appropriate mathematics, on one side and the data obtained by astronomical observation on the other side. This was a particular moment in the history of one dominant natural science, and it set the pattern for the interpretation of natural science as a whole during two centuries. The conception of natural law in Kant and Laplace, and the determinism associated with it, derived their plausibility and their great influence and power from this one astonishing success, which made it seem plausible that a highly abstract explanatory scheme could reliably be combined in all the sciences with faithfulness to observed particularities. We could conclude, without further anxiety, that 'Nature is adapted to our powers of cognition', in Kant's phrase. This confidence in the rule of law, buttressed by the modern study of physics, was also evidently associated with a confidence in monotheism. So Kant could underline the parallel between the lawfulness in the starry heavens above and in the moral law within.

There could be a further evolution in thought following Kant's Copernican revolution, making human demands for intelligibility in nature more problematic, and concomitantly making the universal moral law also problematic. Suppose that attention is turned toward the vast and uncharted turbulences and uncertainties which modern astrophysics reveals, aided by new technologies of observation, and also to the apparent anomalies of quantum mechanics. At the same time, other natural sciences alongside physics, and also new areas of physics, present a bewildering variety of theoretical structures that seem to preclude any easy overview of current natural knowledge as a whole. It then becomes natural to look suspiciously at universalist ethics and at any very general theory of justice, and to question whether the great diversity of forms and of kinds of fairness, and of forms and kinds of substantial justice, are best understood only through a set of general principles. We seem to need complementarily to disperse our attention over a great range of different customs and attitudes and of different moral and political traditions: in the style of Herodotus's history. This dispersed vision of human societies and of languages is also the method, and the approach, of a certain kind of biologist who may be called a naturalist. His interest and his habits of mind are those of a scholar who composes a lexicon for the ancient Greek language. He is a scholar of nature, who would contrast himself with those biologists who study the structures of biochemical processes. The difference between the two interests, particular and general, is evidently not to be identified with a distinction between disciplines: for example, between natural science and human history.

The difference between the two kinds of inquiry is better seen as coming from a difference between the uses and the applications of the two kinds of knowledge pursued. A complete, or nearly complete, catalogue or map of natural kinds of animals and plants has many obvious uses as a repository of knowledge to be drawn on for practical and theoretical purposes. Equally, discovery of the general laws governing the mechanisms of inheritance throughout the biosphere has obvious uses in making possible active interventions in natural processes. The two kinds of investigation are complementary. There is no good reason to regard the

discovery of universal, or very general, natural laws as constituting the only, or the principal, paradigm for moral thinking.
The habits of thought of systematists and of lexicographers
and of cartographers also supply examples that may influence
those who are thinking about justice and morality: not the
habits of mind that lead to the discovery of the means of
intervention in, and control of, natural processes, but the
habit of noticing and recording the full range of particular
cases of natural phenomena with all their various differences
and peculiarities.

If one today takes part in an argumentative political conflict about substantial injustice in the distribution of wealth,
or in access to legal aid, or in the rights of immigrants, one
would certainly look to general principles involved in current
ideas of equality and fairness, but also to the actual or
possible embodiment of these principles in actual known
social systems, including one's own, and in easily imagined
social systems not altogether remote from one's own. In a
preindustrial society, in which large landowners dominated
and in which taxes could not easily be collected, the customary way of life would make many of the now accepted
principles of fairness in taxation unrealisable. The principles
would have no grip on actual practices in the raising of taxes.
In any political process that is designed to eliminate or to
lessen a particular injustice, public argument will revolve
around the plausible analogies between the disputed case and
cases of injustice in the same or a similar domain which are

already recognised. Evidently the arguments will not have anything like the form of a logical demonstration and will not exhibit the rigour of a proof in mathematics. As is characteristic of moral and political and legal arguments, they will be citing evidence and reasons that incline without necessitating.

It will be admitted that the conclusions drawn from such arguments are, in the typical case, properly described as 'matters of opinion', in a context where matters of opinion are contrasted with matters of certain and indisputable knowledge. This has to be admitted, if only because it is indisputable as a fact of observation and of history that such disputes about substantial justice do constantly occur and recur and do provoke arguments of the type described. A consensus, even a temporary and local one, is not easily reached. The disputes unavoidably occur, not only between persons and groups in a public arena, but also in the minds of persons who are thinking about substantial injustices and who must make up their minds in difficult cases: difficult, given their own moral theories and moral outlooks. However bigoted a group of persons may seem, and however strongly they are tied to one particular moral outlook, they will still occasionally meet situations that pose a conflict for them. Then they are compelled to weigh adversary reasons, unless they decide to abandon thought altogether. Even if they renounce all independent thinking about difficult moral and political issues, and simply appeal to some ultimate authority, they will in the ordinary run of affairs employ adversary reasoning, balancing pros and cons of a particular course of action, in difficult prudential cases, and thinking only of self-preservation. The experience of conflict of evidences, whether in their own minds or in discussions with others, is universally shared and cannot be avoided. Even the fanatic who is sure that he knows best in discriminating justice from injustice also knows that he must prepare himself with arguments to meet disagreement.

The pejorative word 'fanatic' brings with it the implication that there can be, and ought to be, a habit of self-questioning in matters of moral and political controversy, and that it is a good thing that this habit should be built into a culture as a part, and as a dominant part, in any modern society. In fact this habit, and its wide dissemination, could be regarded as the defining characteristic of a liberal society. Alongside the undeniable evils of domination and of procedural justice denied, other moral values are in principle open to challenge in liberal societies, even those that are strongly supported by the public opinion of the time. Open debate about competing values is itself a value.

Machiavelli and Hobbes famously insisted that political conflicts are not finally and reliably resolved on a rational level by adversary argument, because they normally also bring with them a struggle for power in the state or in the society, which often overwhelms the rational procedures. Even those whose conception of the good requires that rational procedures of conflict resolution should be stretched as far as they can be must acknowledge that in fact they will often undetermine the outcome: not only for Hobbesian reasons, because of concomitant struggles for sovereignty and power, but also because of the nature of reasoning itself. In mathematics and the natural sciences, in most historical studies and in all scholarship, adversary reasoning in the face of conflicting evidence and rival theories is thought of as an expected stage along the path to an eventual consensus, even if this consensus is later revised or reinterpreted because of new evidence. Our shared conception of the truth in the natural sciences, and in factual inquiries into past events, presupposes this expected convergence. When consensus is achieved, argument ceases. This is the point of contrast between different kinds of reasoning, the convergent and its opposite, reasoning that is inherently disputable.

My conception of good and evil is not a social and public possession, built up cooperatively and cumulatively, and tending toward a final conclusion, with all conflicts resolved. While I live, my conception of good and evil naturally and normally tends to be revised and amplified as my experience and my reflection may suggest. Precisely because my values and goals are guiding my activities and sentiments as my life proceeds, my reflections on virtues and values are kept open, ready for the new evidences of experience, if I am a reflective person. But there is yet another, and perhaps a more funda-mental, reason why conceptions of the good are not formed and supported by convergent reasoning. The values and the virtues, which we review in our own minds and discuss with others, including the virtue of substantial justice, are properly seen as comparative values that have to be placed in an order of priority among a whole set of possible values. We define the values and the virtues, and determine their priority, by reference to the comparative evil of their negations. In day-to-day thinking and acting, and conspicuously in politics, we have to construct an order of priority among evils to be avoided, acquiescing, for example, in minor substantial injustices in order to avoid greater evils of some other kind: for example, greater unhappiness. My conception of the good is the order of priority that I habitually assign to the greater and lesser evils to be avoided in my decision making.

Our moral imaginations stretch far beyond our actual capacities, and we can easily imagine a better life in a better social system, which would involve us in accepting less injustice than we do at present. Perhaps we plot with ourselves, and with political and moral allies, to pick out the greater evils here and now and to assess the true and ultimate cost of avoiding them. This requires a scattered and unregulated kind of reasoning, the style of politicians and of historians, and it is a style of thought that every reasonable man also uses in forming his strictly self-interested policies. It is a calculation of balances of evil within the constraints of practical possibilities.

Within this style of thinking, once its scattered nature is

recognised and accepted, one does not expect to make use of a single all-embracing theory of good and evil, as Aristotle did in the Nicomachean Ethics. Aristotle's theory was as thin and unconstraining as it could be made, allowing for the vast variety of particular cases and singularities that Aristotle knew to be facts of life as we experience them. But there still remained a theory of complete happiness and complete virtue in a complete life, which would temper recognition of the diversity of kinds of virtue and of forms of success and achievement. The old Platonic drive to the single good was still there, because otherwise human aspirations would be 'empty and vain', that is, not certified and fulfilled by an ultimate harmony. The demand for complete intelligibility and for rational coherence was dominant and swept all other considerations out of the way. So it did also later in the Ages of Faith and after the collapse of paganism in the West. An intelligible and coherent account of the Creator and of his Creation carries with it the implication that there can be no inexplicable leaps or gaps in nature, rightly understood. Correspondingly, a rational person's moral theory, including her notion of substantial justice, ought to be seamless and complete, with the relation among the virtues fully explained and yielding a coherent picture of the human good.

The contrary theory of rationality as two-sided adversary reasoning carries with it a contrary metaphysics. A human subject, inheriting and constructing for himself or herself a way of life, including some notions of justice and fairness, is

presumed always to have a narrowly limited range of experience and a narrowly limited range of feeling, together with
some knowledge of the world, knowledge that he recognises
to be at all points incomplete and full of gaps. He has one,
and only one, source of reassurance. He finds that other
persons, to whom he talks and who use the same language as
himself, are in these respects in the same situation as himself.
Some of them recognise and accept the pathos of their
situation, the narrow limits of their experience, of their range
of feeling, of their knowledge of the world, but others do not
and, more pathetic still, suppose themselves to have tran-
scended the limits with some vision of a knowledge of
perfect justice.

Rationality in politics, and hence procedural justice, requires, as a condition of its existence, the convergence of
several minds working together in shared practices. The just
procedures have to be collaborative practices, although the
collaborators allot themselves different, and often adversary,
roles in the process. From the standpoint of an individual,
rationality and fairness in procedure is the habit of examining
particular conflicts and their precedents while shifting one's
perspective on the conflicts by imagining oneself changing
one's role within the process. From the standpoint of society
and of society's necessary mechanisms, that is, of institutions
such as parliaments and law courts, rationality and fairness in
procedure is the custom of providing equal opportunities for
both sides in adversary arguments in all important issues. The

circular processes of rationality, which require that every proposal should provoke the consideration of its denial, are essentially the same process in the social arena and in the individual mind. Plato's inspired analogy between justice in the workings of an individual mind and justice in the city points to the one common and indisputable basis of morality, which makes a bridge between all moral differences in conflict-prone humanity: the habit of argument within the solitary soul that is modelled on the habit of argument within assemblies, committees, and law courts. We are citizens who have a feeling for justice in public affairs because we have faction-ridden souls torn between contrary impulses, and we are persons who are normally in dispute with ourselves. At first hand, we know about the reflective balancing of pros and cons from which we have to construct some degree of consistency in action and in attitude for ourselves, and for this reason we can recognise and respond to the contrarieties of political debate and public argument.

Although a feeling for procedural justice and fairness and for rationality is grounded in human nature, and in the nature of human thought, justice, it must be remembered, has never been thought to be the only virtue, even though it is perhaps the principal virtue in practical affairs and in politics. It is a feature of all political experience that rational procedures, and moral convictions generally, at best go only half the way to explain the attitudes and actions of those who take an active part in great public events, because it is known that

71

there is an uncontrolled element of chance in the outcome of political contests and also because political power and political influence are not to be measured, or even easily to be calculated. The uncertainty and unpredictability, and therefore the difficulties of decision, are normally greater in political conflicts than in a person's conduct of his private life. In the exercise of power on any large scale there are always emergencies arising from the number and diversity of unknown persons and populations involved. The experience of political power is the experience of unplanned responses to emergencies in constant succession. This is Machiavelli's stress on 'Fortuna' as part of the essence of political agency and his consequent stress on the power of decision as a primary virtue peculiar to politics. Political responsibility is in this sense different from moral responsibility. A man or woman who is a leader in his society, and who has a following, owes it to his followers to be decisive and successful, even at the cost of his own integrity and moral respectability. His followers and supporters rely upon him to protect their lives and their freedoms by any lawful means that are available, and it becomes his duty not to falter and not to lose his way and not to be weakened by conflicts in his own mind.

Politicians and statesmen naturally act under the necessity of supporting their own side in contests against its enemies. They fade into ineffectiveness, and will finally disappear from the field altogether, if on every issue they follow their own conception of the good, overriding the desires and opinions of those who have been their allies in the past, and who will be needed as their allies in the future. Evidently they often sacrifice some of their own ideals and moral commitments for the sake of preserving their alliances. They will sometimes allow some part of their own conception of the good to be suspended in practice because their indispensable political friends do not at all points share their conception of the good. For example, I may belong to a political party which permits or encourages procedures for determining citizenship that I regard as substantially unjust and unfair. I may reasonably decide to acquiesce in the injustice, in order to protect other values that, within my conception of the good, are ranked higher. Political casuistry is generally more complex than the casuistry that is required to meet moral dilemmas in private life. Machiavelli stresses and overstresses the claims of political responsibility at the expense of the claims of an individual's moral probity, because Machiavelli's conception of the good puts patriotism and leadership and historical achievement at the head of all the human virtues. Most Christians, and most persons of liberal temperament, do not accept this conception of the good and of its priorities. But all three parties, Machiavellians, serious Christians, and secular liberals, will in any case find themselves entangled in conflicts that will never be resolved into a perfect harmony of values.

III

Conflict and Conflict Resolution

*

Within any nation there will always be contests arising not only from conflicting interests, particularly economic interest, but also from competing moral outlooks and entrenched beliefs. There is one overriding moral principle that every citizen has good reason to accept and to honour in practice: that is the principle of institutionalised fairness in procedures for the resolution of these conflicts. These fair procedures, political and legal, constitute the cement that holds the state together, and supply a common ground of loyalty shared by the citizens who recognise this institutional bond between them: usually weaker in sentiment than the bond of a whole shared moral outlook, or the bonds of kinship, but still a bond that makes itself felt when there is a conflict of loyalties, and when the state has by fair processes arrived at a decision that is morally repugnant to some individual citizens. Domination, the suppression of conflicts by force or by the threat of force, is a great political evil that every citizen may be expected to feel as evil, even if he does not agree with the particular priority given to it among the great evils by his fellow citizens. Even those men of religion who are disgusted by the easygoing tolerance of secular liberals will have a rational ground for respecting the institutions that enable such liberal attitudes and practices to survive alongside their own. The rational ground of respect is rationality itself, the habit of balancing pros and cons in argument, a norm that they cannot without disaster discard in their own thinking.

If I claim that poverty, like disease, or the wounds of war, or imprisonment, or public humiliation, is one of the great evils that afflict human beings, this moral claim will be defended through reference to the actual experience of poverty and to feelings of sympathy and of imaginative identification. This high priority accorded to poverty among evils to be avoided is certainly not universally acceptable as the canons of rational procedure can be. It is part of a particular moral outlook that many moralists of many different persuasions will reject. If I am addressing someone who has not experienced poverty and who cannot imagine the experience of it, or who has no strong feelings of sympathy, my claim will be either denied or brushed aside as politically irrelevant. Such a respondent will agree that poverty is something to be avoided and is in so far evil, but that, considered in the context of political action, the avoidance of it does not have a high priority – partly perhaps because the defence of the state and of individual freedoms ought to have a much higher priority and partly because poverty is essentially a natural, and not a man-made, evil, and therefore is largely outside the proper scope of political action. Politics is the domain of public and responsible choice, and we typically have to choose between war and peace. But it may be argued that we do not choose between famine and plenty, or between the plague and good health, or between sanity and madness. In the centuries of the Christian era before 1848 and the Communist Manifesto, these latter contrasts between good and bad in human experience were taken to lie outside, or at best on the margin, of effective state action or of social planning, and hence outside political argument. Obviously there were at all times glancing sympathetic references to the sufferings of the poor, to famine and disease, and to the moral and theological questions that they suggest. So in Swift's *A Modest Proposal* or, surprisingly, in *Les Caractères* of La Bruyère in the seventeenth century, or later in Samuel Johnson's reported feelings for the poor, there is a vivid sense of the great evil of poverty, but much less sense of the evil as a political reality, comparable with the evils of tyranny and of lawlessness. Then with Jacobinism and Napoleon's social policies and with Bentham's utilitarian philosophy, the age of proactive politics began: the proper range of political argument was being gradually extended throughout the nineteenth century.

The aim of the socialist movement throughout the century, and after the Communist Manifesto of 1848, was to extend the recognised sphere of political action to include the whole of 'the condition of the people,' as the current phrase went in Britain: the poverty and deprivation of the unprivileged, the conditions of work in factories and farms, child labour, public health and nutrition, standards in housing and education. Over the years all these elements in the quality of life of working people were to be moved into the public domain and to be made a field of political conflict.

The essence of socialism as a moral and political theory, discernible in all its many varieties, is the commitment to political agency far beyond the domain recognised in earlier centuries and in other political philosophies. Political institutions and political actions must in the modern world become the first resource for counteracting the great evils, in the place of religious institutions and their charities. The original appeal of socialism in the work of Karl Marx was to an aggressive and more practical humanism, which intended to redraw the boundary between natural and man-made evils, and to bring many more of the sources of human suffering and frustration into the political domain. The political forces resisting socialism have always tried to defend the previously recognised boundary between natural and man-made evils, arguing their case with an ideology that stresses the freedom of the individual and the threat to freedom of enlarged powers for the state. Phrases such as 'the nanny state' are now used by those advocating a morality that gives priority to the autonomy of the individual and to the virtues of self-reliance and of enterprise at the expense of organised public benevolence.

Both sides in this clash of moralities, long-running in the developed world, call upon a supporting ideology, each invoking different conceptions of freedom. The adversary reasoning engendered by these competing moralities with their attached ideologies has been the stuff of democratic politics in the twentieth century. From the point of view of a liberal democrat, this may be a reason for complacency as long as fair procedures of dispute and conflict are preserved. Within a person's morality as a typical liberal, as opposed to a conservative or a socialist, the fact that a particular set of policies – for example, those establishing the welfare state – has emerged victorious from a fair political battle is sufficient ground for affirming the acceptability of these policies. For a typical liberal democrat, as I interpret him, the fact that a particular policy is the outcome of a fair process of democratic conflict is both a necessary and a sufficient condition of its acceptability. For a democratic socialist, and for typical British conservatives, that the policy is the outcome of a fair and established procedure of conflict resolution is a necessary, but certainly not a sufficient, condition of its acceptability. If the finally chosen policy seems to me extremely and evidently unjust in substance, it will often be in my view unacceptable. When a policy seems to me unacceptable, what form my opposition to it should take is a separate moral question, to be determined in the particular circumstances and in view of the extent of the evil.

The arguments around the extended role of the state, and about the scope of collective and political action, raise issues that are properly philosophical, if they are pressed far enough. Those who want to give priority to the autonomy of individuals, and to their unfettered control over their own lives, probably do not think of persons as entirely natural objects whose activities are to be wholly explicable in terms of natural causes. For them the absolute value of human life, peculiar to this unique species, resides in a person's power of thoughtful self-direction. If we do not give free play to this power before everything else, they will argue that we are left with no absolute value to be recognised in the world, and that therefore we must fall back on the various values that different cultures and different persons, subject to ascertainable influences, now happen to accept.

This is a coherent argument, more powerfully stated by Kant, but also, in different forms and with many modifications, widely disseminated and recognised in pre-philosophical opinions. Christian moralists, and other monotheists, insist on the responsibility of human beings for the evil that they do and that they consequently suffer, a responsibility that is unique, and that sets them above and apart from other creatures in the natural order.

This is a philosophy that accords overriding moral priority to individuals and to the authority of their practical reasoning. Of lower priority are the collective decisions of institutions and of social groups, as opposed to individuals, and of lower priority also are the sentiments, desires, and interests that a person happens to have, as opposed to the supposed universal moral principles by which any truly rational person will be guided. This appeal to universal principles has been one of the philosophical backgrounds to liberal attitudes in politics, and it stands in direct line of descent from Protestant stress on the individual citizen's conscience as the principal arbiter under God in all moral issues, private or public. A contrary philosophy of mind and of personality, one of many, assumes that the sentiments and desires, reflective and unreflective, of persons determine their conduct together with the calculations that occur in their practical reasoning. Their sentiments and desires may be considered admirable or the reverse from one or another moral standpoint, and their practical adversary reasoning may be reasonable or unreasonable. But no claim is made for the autonomy of the individual's will as something that stands outside the natural order, and that has a unique and absolute value. This philosophy asserts that no feature of personality stands outside the natural order, and that natural sentiments and emotions, refined both by reflection and by specific customs, are the source and the ground of substantial moral values. Only the principle of fairness in settling conflicts can claim a universal ground as being a principle of shared rationality, indispensable in all decision making and in all intentional action.

From this naturalistic standpoint the interferences of a

socialist state in the lives of its citizens, and some loss of self-direction, have to be weighted as being so far negative against the gains in welfare and a sense of security. We naturalists argue that there are no absolute values involved in this conflict, and that the work of practical reason is the balancing of the different evils to be avoided. The line separating man-made evils from evils that come from the nature of things is a fluctuating line and is determined as much by our actions, and by our conceived possibilities of action, as by our observations. If we successfully develop the social practices and the technologies that will anticipate and prevent the occurrence of famines, famines are moved into the column of man-made evils, insofar as, on particular occasions, a famine is traceable to avoidable faults in these practices. Once the national health service exists, and cosmetic surgery is among its skills, then harelips and squints, common in earlier populations, become more than natural misfortunes, to be acquiesced in. They become a politically accepted cost in some preferred allocation of resources, if they are not corrected.

The socialist programme in the nineteenth century required a new aggressive political consciousness engendered in the mass of working people, and it required also fitting institutions, conspicuously trade unions, that would incorporate this new agency and would assume leadership. Unlike the leading thinkers of the Enlightenment, socialists were not thinking of themselves as solving social problems objectively defined, and presented by the condition of the people, but rather as creating for working men the best attainable conditions of life and work through consolidating their mastery of political processes. It was their duty as socialists to cause urban and rural poverty to be seen as an immediate problem for politicians, rather than as a misfortune that occurs naturally, like bad weather. They should think of themselves as organising their supporters for conflict, because tolerable conditions of life and work would never be conceded to them without a political conflict. The end and purpose of the conflict, which was the emancipation of the workers, would emerge from the conflict itself. It was, they thought, an illusion to suppose that some general principles of distributive justice could be effectively invoked to settle disputes about fair wages and decent conditions of work. This was the liberal hope, at once false and debilitating: false, because no universally acceptable premises exist from which the alleged principles can be deduced; debilitating, because such a hope will undermine the need for aggressive political organisation in readiness for conflict when consensus has predictably proved unattainable.

The inevitability of political conflict over distributive justice and fair conditions of employment is from the beginning assumed in socialist theory. In any exchange and whatever the commodity exchanged, the buyers and the vendors have conflicting interests in settling the price. This remains true when the commodity in exchange is labour, and when the buyers are those who have access to capital and those offering their labour do not. The resulting conflict over labour costs is expressed at a political level in adversary arguments circling around principles of justice and fairness of reward. The rival notions of justice and fairness are not a priori stipulations; the arguments on both sides are constrained by customary and previously known, even if disputable, notions of distributive justice, each side selectively quoting in debate those already accepted notions that support its case. At the level of political argument, within the institutions fulfilling this function, each side presents its claim under the heading, and in the guise, of notions of fairness, rather than as un-adorned self-interest. For example, the capitalists will point to the unfairness of inadequate compensation for financial risk, and the workers will point to the unfairness of inadequate compensation for the hardship and the monotony of the work.

Those who have access to capital and to wealth in excess of immediate needs will tend to support the conceptions of distributive justice already prevailing in their society. They will tend to see these conceptions as timeless truths or self-evident principles of justice, even though the timeless truths in fact emerge from earlier contests and from temporary settlements. On the conservative side advocacy will point to the value of stability and to the authority of customary moral ideas, including ideas of distributive justice, while advocacy on the reforming side will point to the contingent history of these ideas. Reformers will usually argue that the distribution of advantages in accordance with prevailing notions of justice is perpetually in need of revision and criticism, if only because the perceived social roles of different classes and groups in society are constantly changing. To take a drastically simplified example: when the survival of a society or state was perceived to depend on the successes and efforts of a warrior class, it would be accepted as fair that members of this class should as a reward have exceptional advantages and privileges. When this service becomes only a memory, the privileges come to seem unfair and unjustifiable. But no general principle of fairness can be formulated linking the vastly various types of service to the vastly various types of acceptable reward. One can only observe in history that privileges often come to be resented, and to be felt to be unjustifiable, when the social role with which they were associated has disappeared, or when for other reasons it is no longer respected. The inequality is then felt to be unfair. This is an observable natural tendency of reflective sentiment, which affects the fate of monarchies and of aristocracies and of élites of other kinds, including the agents of colonial powers.

Fairness in distributive justice is recognised when there is a rough convergence of reflective human feeling, a convergence that is never perfect, and that always leaves exceptions and uncertainties. This is why questions of fairness in the distribution of goods and of penalties are always matters of opinion and often give rise to conflicts. But it is a necessity, and not a matter of opinion, that such conflicts should be resolved either by argument or by force. About this necessity there cannot be two opinions among practically reasoning persons who, aware of contrary impulses in their own minds, are accustomed to weighing the pros and cons as fairly as they can. In the balancing of pros and cons in situations of inner conflict, we come to a resting place unless and until further considerations suggest themselves; so also in the public and political domain. At this point fairness and two-sidedness in the thoughtful balancing come together with rationality. For this reason there is a point of overlap and a coming together between conservative political groups and reforming or progressive political groups, when they each present the arguments supporting their policies in the adversary form characteristic of their own private thinking. On both sides of the barricades, conservative and reformist, everyone has adversaries within his own soul and is in this way already prepared to step out onto the political or legal stage and to argue his case. He has already rehearsed the fairness of a statement followed by a rebuttal, followed by restatement, in his own thinking. If he and his adversary abstain from force, they both know the rational procedure that remains.

Rationality is a bond between persons, but it is not a very powerful bond, and it is apt to fail as a bond when there are strong passions on two sides of a conflict. What sentiment

can reinforce the bond in a conflict where there are passion-
ate loyalties on both sides? What could possibly be an
overriding loyalty that will preserve the institutions of fair
adversary reasoning when they are tested in a bitter conflict
of values? it seems that any political philosophy needs to
have an answer to this question, not least a philosophy that
stresses the inevitability and desirability of political conflict.
Within the limits of my argument the answer can be found
only in institutional loyalties and in deep-seated habits of
living together and arguing together. Famously, family
conventions and habits of conversation and family under-
standings can often survive appalling moral conflicts, and
families are the model to which other quasi-intimate institutions are expected to approximate: churches, clubs, colleges,
schools, tribes, parishes, each with its traditional customs and
loyalties. For the modern nation-state the nearest, but still
very distant, equivalent is the inherited constitution with the
more prominent, and the longer-established, institutions that
are long-lasting parts of the constitution. In the United States
very bitter conflicts of moral principle, involving substantially different conceptions of substantial justice, have been
resolved argumentatively by the Supreme Court of the
United States, and the Supreme Court has been both the
setting and the mechanism of the conflict resolution. The
Court and its procedures have in fact acquired authority and
have established a tradition of respect among bitter adversaries contesting substantive issues of justice. No one is

expected to believe that its decisions are infallibly just in matters of substance; but everybody is expected to believe that at least its procedures are just because they conform to the basic principle governing adversary reasoning: that both sides in a conflict should be equally heard. The procedures by which the justices are originally appointed are the ordinary procedures by which officeholders are usually appointed in a democracy, and they make no special claim to be just procedures. But the conventions that govern the advocacy on both sides in a case before the Supreme Court arise from a specific conception of justice: that arguments, to be persuasive, must appeal to commonly and customarily accepted ideas of substantial justice relevant to the case, but also to relevant precedents in past decisions of the Court. The persuasive force of this appeal to precedent is a natural consequence of one-half of the composite notion of procedural justice; the other half, equality in adversary reasoning, is secured by the constitution of the Court itself as a deliberative body.

In parliaments, councils, and governmental bodies of all kinds, the two elements of procedural justice are differently balanced. The requirement that both sides in the conflict should be equally heard always needs to be stressed because it is not obviously guaranteed, as it is in a court of law. Conflicts that are resolved in parliaments and governmental bodies of all kinds normally involve political and ideological enemies arguing against each other, and not professional advocates who at the same time acknowledge a common allegiance to the law of the land. Every appeal to precedent in a political procedural dispute, and every appeal to equality of access, is open to dispute, if it is not already guaranteed by the undisputed law of the land. So disputes about the just and fair political procedures and institutions will continue indefinitely, punctuated by occasional compromises. No finality or conclusiveness in this historical process is to be expected. Although many of the procedures of political conflict resolution are laid down by law in the American written Constitution, it is evident that some procedures of conflict resolution do in fact significantly change from decade to decade as a consequence of the political conflicts, and also because of changing circumstances. This is also true of Britain's unwritten constitution, although it still embodies parliamentary methods of conflict resolution that have been remarkably slow to change over the last half century.

The two elements in procedural justice – a universal rational requirement of two-sidedness and respect for locally established and familiar rules of procedure – are linked as two natural needs in our minds in their practical and political workings. If either the rational requirement or the respect for custom breaks down and ceases to operate, we should expect catastrophe. Conflicts will then no longer be resolved within the political domain but will be resolved by violence or the threat of violence, and life will become nasty, brutish, and

91

short. Whatever one's conception of the good, such anarchy will generally be reckoned a great evil, alongside starvation and near-starvation, disease, imprisonment, slavery, and humiliation.

Index